The Chinese Americans

MARISSA LINGEN

WE CAME TO AMERICA

MASON CREST PUBLISHERS • PHILADELPHIA

Begun around 221 B.C., the Great Wall of China is the largest engineering and building project ever carried out in the history of humankind. Originally intended to protect the newly united country against invading nomads, the wall today is one of the world's most popular tourist attractions.

The Chinese Americans

MARISSA LINGEN

WE CAME TO AMERICA

MASON CREST PUBLISHERS • PHILADELPHIA

Mason Crest Publishers
370 Reed Road
Broomall PA 19008
www.masoncrest.com

First printing

1 3 5 7 9 8 6 4 2

Library of Congress Cataloging-in-Publication Data
on file at the Library of Congress

ISBN 1-59084-108-5

Table of Contents

WE CAME TO AMERICA

America's Ethnic Heritage

Barry Moreno, librarian

Statue of Liberty/

Ellis Island National Monument

E thnic diversity is one of the most striking characteristics of the American identity. In the United States the Bureau of the Census officially recognizes 122 different ethnic groups. North America's population had grown by leaps and bounds, starting with the American Indian tribes and nations—the continent's original people—and increasing with the arrival of the European colonial migrants who came to these shores during the 16th and 17th centuries. Since then, millions of immigrants have come to America from every corner of the world.

But the passage of generations and the great distance of America from the "Old World"—Europe, Africa, and Asia—has in some cases separated immigrant peoples from their roots. The struggle to succeed in America made it easy to forget past traditions. Further, the American spirit of freedom, individualism, and equality gave Americans a perspective quite different from the view of life shared by residents of the Old World.

Immigrants of the 19th and 20th centuries recognized this at once. Many tried to "Americanize" themselves by tossing away their peasant clothes and dressing American-style even before reaching their new homes in the cities or the countryside of America. It was not so easy to become part of America's culture, however. For many immigrants, learning English was quite a hurdle. In fact, most older immigrants clung to the old ways, preferring to speak their native languages and follow their familiar customs and traditions. This was easy to do when ethnic neighborhoods abounded in large North American cities like New York, Montreal, Philadelphia, Chicago, Toronto, Boston, Cleveland, St. Louis, New Orleans and San Francisco. In rural areas, farm families—many of them Scandinavian, German, or Czech—established their own tightly knit communities. Thus foreign languages and dialects, religious beliefs, Old World customs, and certain class distinctions flourished.

The most striking changes occurred among the children of immigrants, whose hopes and dreams were different from those of their parents. They began breaking away from the Old World customs, perhaps as a reaction to the embarrassment of being labeled "foreigner." They badly wanted to be Americans, and assimilated more easily than their parents and grandparents. They learned to speak English without a foreign accent, to dress and act like other Americans. The assimilation of the children of immigrants was encouraged by social contact—games, schools, jobs, and military service—which further broke down the barriers between immigrant groups and hastened the process of Americanization. Along the way, many family traditions were lost or abandoned.

Today, the pride that Americans have in their ethnic roots is one of the abiding strengths of both the United States and Canada. It shows that the theory which called America a "melting pot" of the world's people was never really true. The thought that a single "American" would emerge from the combination of these peoples has never happened, for Americans have grown more reluctant than ever before to forget the struggles of their ethnic forefathers. The growth of cultural studies and genealogical research indicates that Americans are anxious not to entirely lose this identity, whether it is English, French, Chinese, African, Mexican, or some other group. There is an interest in tracing back the family line as far as records or memory will take them. In a sense, this has made Americans a divided people; proud to be Americans, but proud also of their ethnic roots.

As a result, many Americans have welcomed a new identity, that of the hyphenated American. This unique description has grown in usage over the years and continues to grow as more Americans recognize the importance of family heritage. In the end, this is an appreciation of America's great cultural heritage and its richness of its variety.

1 Secrets and Snakeheads

Immigration from China to the United States has never been easy. During the 19th century the United States passed strict laws that did not allow Chinese people into the country. At this time, most Chinese *immigrants* were working too hard to spend much time recording their experiences, so outside sources and formal poems are the only way people today can learn about their experiences.

After the U.S. decided to let more Chinese people into the country during the mid-20th century, a *communist* government came to power in China. It did not want any of its citizens to leave. China's immigration policies have changed many times since the Communist Party took power, but all of them have been harsh. Many Chinese Americans have stories to tell about arriving in the United States, but they are afraid to give their names, for fear that their relatives still living in China will suffer.

Since ancient times, the Chinese made paper and wooden images of the dragon god and paraded them through the streets to petition for rain. The tradition remains a popular part of Chinese New Year celebrations. These people are carrying the world's longest Chinese dragon during a procession in Honolulu, Hawaii.

One girl from the town of Changle told the story of how she came to America in the mid-1990s. She would only give her name as "Niu." She had high hopes for the new country. Her whole life centered around being an American. "I thought that if I ever had the opportunity to come to the United States, my life would not be wasted. Because so many people from my area have come to America, if I didn't, I would have been looked down on by others. My neighbors would have thought that everyone in my family was useless."

Most Chinese people try to immigrate with their families. However, Niu's parents did not want to come with her. Nor did they want her to go. She had to create major problems in her family to be allowed to leave. "When I told my parents I wanted to go to America, they were against it because I was so young," she said. "Then I started creating problems at home, like frequently arguing with my parents. Soon they were convinced that they had no choice but to let me go."

Niu was only able to come to America because she had wealthy relatives in both China and America. The cost of her journey was high. Like many Chinese immigrants, she took an indirect route so that she would be harder to trace.

First, she got information from some friends about **recruiters,** called "little snakeheads." "They said I only had to pay a little snakehead about $60 and he would allow me to board the ship," she explained. "No need to provide anything else. My friends also said I would need to pay a big snakehead $30,500 when I reached the

Rice is an important crop in China, as in many Asian countries. It is also a staple in the Chinese diet. The land where rice is to be cultivated is usually flooded with 2 to 4 inches of water, since rice paddies thrive under water. Though it is time-consuming and messy, harvesting is often still done by hand.

United States." The little snakehead was the man who would get her out of China. The big snakehead was the man who would get her into the United States.

At age 14, Niu left her parents' home and took a ship to Hong Kong. There she paid the little snakehead and met up with the big snakehead. The big snakehead helped Niu travel from Hong Kong to Thailand to Paris and finally to New York, where her relatives were waiting for her. Like many Chinese immigrants before her, she was young and scared. She broke several laws in getting to the United States. But like many Chinese immigrants before her, Niu decided that the rewards of American life were greater than the risks. ✳

Shoppers crowd the sidewalk of Toronto's Chinatown neighborhood. In many major cities, these sections are often popular, vibrant, and self-sustaining business districts.

2 A Few At A Time

It is hard to determine who the first Chinese people in the New World were. Some settlers with Spanish-sounding names were actually Chinese people. They had first immigrated to the Philippines, and some had taken on Spanish names to fit in with the culture of the islands, which were ruled by Spain during the 16th century. They came with Spanish and Philippine sailors to settle the west coast of North America, from northern California to Mexico. One of the founders of Los Angeles was a Chinese man named Antonio Rodriguez.

There are no good records of how many Chinese settlers came to Mexico. It's clear that there were many in the early years. Acapulco had so many Chinese people in it that it was called *ciudad de los Chinos*, the city of the Chinese. In Mexico City in 1635, the Chinese barbers were so numerous and successful that Spanish barbers successfully lobbied to have them kicked out.

Because China is a Communist country, the government can regulate more aspects of everyday life than democratic governments such as the United States do. Because of the high population density of China, for instance, families are supposed to have only one child each.

The Chinese emperor had declared hundreds of years before that anyone who **emigrated** from China and came back would have his head cut off. While this law was not well enforced, it was still on the books. It indicated how little chance Chinese immigrants had of being accepted back into Chinese society in the 1600s and 1700s. North America didn't get too many Chinese immigrants during this time. As restrictions in China eased, immigrants came more freely, starting in the late 1700s.

Chinese labor played a key role in the early days of colonization of the Pacific coast of North America. In 1788, Chinese laborers built a fort for the British in Nootka Sound on Vancouver Island. The fort was eventually abandoned, however, and more than 100 Chinese people dispersed into the wilderness of the Northwestern coast.

It was not until the Gold Rush of 1849 that Chinese people started coming to North America in consistently large numbers. At first, the white people in California were glad to see the Chinese. It was hard to get supplies shipped all the way out to California from the settled eastern states, so Chinese merchants were welcomed with open arms. They brought food, tools, utensils, textiles, and even **prefabricated** housing materials for the California settlers.

California citizens made a big deal out of welcoming the new Chinese arrivals in the first few years. Chinese **delegations** were invited to march in parades, and there were ceremonies to meet the first ships of Chinese people. There was even a Chinese delegation in the festivities celebrating California's statehood in 1850. Unfortunately, the good relations between Chinese and white people only lasted for a few years.

Soon, educated Chinese people realized they had other opportunities within the new Californian settlements. Some of the

Chefs work in the kitchen of a restaurant in New York's Chinatown. Chinese restaurants have steadily grown in popularity since the time of the California Gold Rush, when Americans first tasted the exotic food of the Far East.

Asian and Latino workers pause in a field during the grape harvest in California. Even if they were skilled laborers, many Chinese immigrants were forced to do grueling migrant work to make a living.

people who came were doctors, engineers, merchants, and smiths. One of the most popular professions was that of a carpenter. Carpenters were needed to put together the prefabricated houses for the new California residents. The most **prestigious** people—the scholars and the elders—almost never came to America, but many members of the middle classes did.

The Chinese population of California increased by almost 20,000 in the three years after the beginning of the Gold Rush. Eighty percent of this population was from the province of Kwangtung, also called Guangdong or Canton. This proportion still holds true of Chinese Americans today: More than 80 percent have Cantonese ancestry.

Because most of the Chinese people who came to America at first were educated and fairly well-off, their voyage to America was much nicer than the average European immigrant's. Crowded steamships were rare. For the most part, Chinese immigrants paid reasonable prices for decent conditions—small, clean staterooms on board the ships.

In 1850, Hawaii was still a separate country, the Kingdom of Hawaii. The king of Hawaii knew that the native Hawaiian population was declining. At the same time, the Hawaiian economy was booming. He decided to open Hawaii to Chinese laborers. While some opposed it, most Hawaiians accepted Chinese workers with open arms. Chinese and native Hawaiians intermarried. To this day, Hawaii is one of the most ethnically integrated parts of the

United States, with Chinese, Hawaiian, Japanese, Filipino, and white Americans intermingling thoroughly.

The poorer day-laborers who left China were mostly moving to the Dutch colonies in the East Indies. But it was only a matter of time before the need for labor would draw more workers to the United States and Canada. During the 1840s, China was fighting a war with England, and many people in the U.S. still resented British *colonialism*. Later, American-British relations started to improve, so the Chinese lost their image as a brave people fighting the colonialist British. Still, it was not until Chinese laborers started to work in the gold mines of California that the relationship between Chinese and whites turned sour. ✸

LUE GIM GONG

In 1872, a 12-year-old boy named Lue Gim Gong came from China without either of his parents. He tried to find work in city industries and factories, but the only employment he could find was in a dank shoe mill. There he developed tuberculosis, a disease of the lungs. He made friends with Miss Fanny Burlingame, an American woman, but went back to China to try to cure his lungs.

Two years later, Miss Burlingame wrote to Lue Gim Gong asking if he wanted to live in her Florida estates, where the air would be better for his lungs. Lue accepted, and it was the start of a notable career in *botany*. Miss Burlingame's home had extensive greenhouses, so the sickly young man could experiment with the plants.

As Lue got older, his experiments began to pay off. He developed what was then called the "love apple" into the regularly sized and shaped tomato that we eat today. He also bred Asian oranges with the European kind to produce a hardy American variety. Using *hybridization*, he developed new types of cherries, celery, teas, and asparagus as well as working with the tomatoes and oranges until they were common, everyday American food.

Chinese laborers pose during the construction of the Northern Pacific Railroad. Chinese men were among the most dependable workers because of their eating habits and hygene. These made them less likely to get sick and miss work.

3 Railroads and Mines

Chinese people had been immigrating to Borneo to work in gold mines for generations. In fact, they had become expert gold miners. When California had its Gold Rush, many of these Chinese people knew that they could do the mining work well. The laboring classes came to California more and more. California became known as Gum Shan, the Gold Mountain.

By 1850, one-third of the gold miners in California were Chinese. White miners became resentful because Chinese miners knew more about mining than they did. Often, a white miner would abandon a claim, thinking that all the gold was gone. Chinese miners would then come in and find more gold. White miners would get mad and chase the Chinese people away from the claims that the Chinese people had staked, even if no white people had been working on them before.

In around the same time period, the railroads grew at a tremendous rate. Workers were desperately needed. Chinese laborers found out about this need and moved to America in large numbers. There were 13,000 Chinese workers on the transcontinental railroad alone.

Railroad crews were often *segregated* by ethnic groups. There would be a Chinese crew, an Irish crew, a German crew, and so on. The Chinese crews cooked their own food using dried imported Chinese ingredients. They were generally faster workers than the other crews, and so they again faced jealousy and resentment. Chinese crews were forced to travel in third class "immigrant cars" when the railroad sent them anywhere.

Along the railroad tracks, villages sprang up. The Chinese usually lived in a Chinese village next to the white village, but was not officially a part of it. This was fine with the Chinese. They wanted to be independent of the white village and had doctors and merchants of their own. Many white settlers had to go to the Chinese doctors for medical care.

After the gold mines of California were exhausted and the railroad had been built, the Chinese workers had to find other jobs in America. Many of them worked on ranches as cowboys. Chinese workers were particularly well-liked by the ranchers' wives because they cooked for themselves instead of making their boss' wife cook.

Cigar-making was a common trade after the railroad and mining work became scarce. Some Chinese people became vegetable *peddlers*. Others founded the Pacific fishing industry. At that time, many white people considered fish an inferior food. Beef and beans were considered a white man's food. The Chinese people liked to eat fish, and a fisherman could almost always feed himself.

At first, fine mesh nets and other fishing gear were imported from China. Later, Chinese Americans made their own nets. Some whites, especially in San Francisco and Los Angeles, did not think the Chinese ought to be so successful with their fishing businesses. They came up with excuses to *levy* special taxes and licenses on the Chinese fishers.

A Chinese man handles a shovel while his partner pans a stream looking for gold nuggets. The forty-niners often resented the Chinese, Mexicans, and other immigrants, because they didn't want "foreigners" finding "their" gold.

In the 1870s, a movement started to **ban** fine mesh nets, which were only used by Chinese fishers. This movement was eventually successful.

Virtually all Chinese immigrants were adult men. Chinese women were treated unfairly. They could be accused of **immoral** behavior and **deported** to China at any time. It was also difficult for Chinese women to get permission to enter the United States or Canada. Early Chinese-American communities were different from any other community of immigrants because they were almost completely comprised of single men.

Chinese fishing nets hover over the water at sunset. Fishing has been important to the people of China for centuries. It is still done using traditional methods.

Children born in the United States were considered precious. Chinese-American girls were more highly valued than girls were in China, because there were so few Chinese-American women. Chinese Americans tried to send their daughters to school in Hong Kong so that they would keep Chinese customs. This practice could be dangerous, however. If their daughters met and married Chinese men, some U.S.

judges ruled that the daughters lost American citizenship and could not enter the country any more.

Another problem for women immigrants was that China still allowed the practice of **bigamy** at that time, although few actually practiced it. Bigamy is when a man has two wives. Sometimes, if immigration officials wanted to deport a woman, they would claim that she was a second wife and thus not legally a wife at all in America.

Many Chinese immigrants kept their wives and children in China. They visited their families as often as they could, not more often than every few years. One of the most embarrassing questions you could ask a Chinese immigrant was, "How many times have you been back to China?" The poorest immigrants could not afford even one trip back to China, and they were ashamed at not getting to see their families.

America was not seen as a final destination by many of the Chinese people who first came here to work. Instead, they intended to earn money so that they and their families could live better in China. When they got to America, however, many found that they couldn't afford to move back to China permanently. Some made arrangements to send their bones back to China to be buried with their ancestors' if they died in America.

To handle problems in the new Chinese-American communities, immigrants formed *huiguans. Huiguan* was a Chinese word for "meeting hall." More often, the members would use English words, calling their huiguan a "company" or an "association." Almost all Chinese Americans in the cities were members of what came to be known as the Six Companies.

The companies did many things. They provided loans to their members and help when illnesses struck. They sometimes funded the shipment of bones back to China. Companies also made sure that Chinese Americans who left for China had paid all their debts in America. They issued slips of paper to their members if their members had cleared all their debts. Ship captains had formed an agreement with the companies and would not take a Chinese person on board unless he had his slip of paper.

One of the things that made the U.S. government angry with the companies was that they served as judicial systems for Chinese immigrants. Chinese people could not testify in American courts because racist laws considered them members of one of the "inferior races." Since they couldn't testify, they often chose to take disputes to the companies instead. The leaders of the company, prominent merchants, would listen to both sides of a story and make a decision, just like any other court.

Although there were still some old regional rivalries left over from their days in China, the Six Companies were mostly peaceful. They were not like the tongs. The tongs were secret societies whose major aim was to run criminal activities. They were descended from the infamous Triad gangs in China and Southeast Asia.

In addition to tongs and companies, there were two other types of clubs that were common in the early days of Chinese-American life. The first was the *gongsi fang*. A gongsi fang was composed of people who were related through their father's side of the family. There were usually no more than 50 people in a gongsi fang. They provided social centers and temporary places for their members to live as well as small loans of money. Gongsi fangs were also called "surname associations." (A surname is a person's family name.)

There were other secret societies that had no name, but were not criminal organizations like the tongs. These were just clubs that appealed to working men for social activities. All these clubs substituted as much as possible for family life among the Chinese immigrants. Since there were few women, the men needed some kind of social life. After the Exclusion Acts ended, however, most of these societies ended as well.

There were several festivals the Chinese-American population brought with them from China. The most popular were the Harvest Moon Festival and the Chinese New Year. The Harvest Moon Festival celebrated the fruits of the year's farming. The Chinese New Year was observed with parades, costumes, gifts, and firecrackers. There were also memorial days when Chinese people observed their ancestors' memories.

One of the most popular activities among Chinese people in America was gambling. In traditional Chinese society, sports and athletic pursuits were considered childish. Also, after a long day's work, many workers were too tired to play sports. Games like stud poker, dominoes, fan tan, blackjack, dice, keno, and chuck-a-luck were popular.

Gambling was considered outside the law in Chinese society. It was illegal to run a gambling parlor in America, but many Chinese people were unaware of that law or did not think it applied to their activities. Many legitimate businessmen also ran gambling houses on the side, and recent immigrants had difficulty finding employment anywhere else until they knew at least a little English. Chinese games were all perfectly fair, but the gambling house took a portion of anything anyone won under their roof.

Gambling was one of the largest reasons white Americans thought that Chinese people were immoral. The other stereotype that worked against the Chinese people from the earliest days was the problem of opium use. Opium was a popular drug at the time, and it was used by whites and Chinese alike. Opium remained legal until 1906, but many recognized it as a social problem long before it was illegal.

Opium *imports* were heavily taxed. Some immigrants attempted to smuggle opium into the U.S. so that they could sell it and have some money to start out with in their new country. (The soles of shoes were favorite hiding places for opium packets.) Other immigrants tried to smuggle in bits of silk, which was highly prized and also heavily taxed. If someone was caught smuggling, he was sent back to China immediately. Immigration officials looking for smuggled opium or silk destroyed many innocent immigrants' personal belongings as the relations between white and Chinese people got more and more shaky. ✺

A parade for the Chinese New Year makes its way through the streets of New York's Chinatown. Since the Chinese calendar follows the phases of the moon, it does not match the Western calendar. Therefore, Chinese New Year falls on a different date each year.

This photo, taken in 1925, shows Chinese men being arrested for possible deportation. If the men cannot prove their citizenship they will be sent back to China. Discriminatory laws and practices made life in America a difficult and anxious experience for Chinese immigrants, even those who had been living in the United States for many years.

4 The Problem Years

Chinese people were called "Celestials" by those who wanted to be polite to them. The emperor of China was called "the Emperor of Heaven," and other aspects of the Chinese empire were referred to in heavenly terms.

For those who didn't mind being rude, however, they were "the heathen Chinee." The Chinese were resented because they had come from a complex and ancient civilization with traditions and religions of their own. Most Americans were frightened and ignorant of non-Christian religions, although a few were intrigued by Chinese culture. Chinese Americans who converted to Christianity were slightly more accepted by middle- and upper-class people, but they were still **patronized** and mocked in many circles.

Being made fun of was the least of a Chinese immigrant's problems. The dominant white culture still did not regard Chinese people as equal human beings. This meant that Chinese people could be attacked, beaten, and even killed, and their tormentors would go free. A vast majority of white people who murdered Chinese immigrants were never even charged with a crime. If a Chinese person did survive an attack, he could not testify in court against his attacker, so he had to depend on a white person to have seen the problem and be willing to step forward.

On the frontier, the U.S. Cavalry would not defend Chinese workers against Native American attacks. Railmen and ranchers often kept guards, but their guards did not protect Chinese workers, either. Many Chinese had to become friendly with Native Americans in their region out of self-defense. This made their bosses suspicious. They were often accused of being in league with the Indians.

Chinese immigrants sometimes married Native American women and tried to pass for Native Americans. They thought they would run into less *prejudice* if they lived in the Native American villages and reservations than if they tried to live with white people. Also, there were almost no Chinese women immigrants, and Chinese men were not legally allowed to marry European-American women. If they wanted to get married, Native American women were their only choice.

There were all sorts of barriers to Chinese people joining normal American society. In 1854, Chinese-American children were classified with African-American and Native American children as "inferior races" and barred from the schools.

Chinese people got blamed as a group for anything bad that happened. One night in 1871 in Los Angeles, 20 innocent Chinese men were hanged or burned alive. Some of them had been spending the evening inside quietly. They were dragged out of their homes and killed for no reason other than the fact they were Chinese.

In mining country, there was resentment from white miners because the Chinese miners almost never wanted to go on strike. In Rock Springs, Wyoming, in 1885, 28 Chinese men were murdered or

This illustration, published by Currier and Ives in 1871, was originally titled "The Heathen Chinee." The prevailing attitude toward Chinese immigrants at the time was that they were ruthlessly cheating gamblers, not to be trusted.

mutilated because they didn't want to strike against the mine owners. None of their killers was ever caught or tried for that crime. The slightest excuse was enough to trigger massacres of Chinese people.

The conditions in Canada were just as bad as in the United States. They also followed a similar pattern: the western provinces, particularly British Columbia, had the worst attitudes towards Chinese people. There was more violence and bloodshed in the west. The western provinces did most of the lobbying to exclude Chinese people by law as well.

In 1879, the people who wrote the California State Constitution tried to prohibit Chinese people from working for white people.

Chinese people were also not allowed to hold government jobs. There were even provisions in the state constitution for removing Chinese people from the state of California.

The ballots on the California State Constitution provisions against Chinese people were highly unfair. There was a space to vote *against* Chinese immigration, but no space to vote *for* Chinese immigration. Fortunately, this part of the state constitution

The pagoda-shaped "Hop Louie" restaurant is a popular hot spot of Chinatown in Los Angeles.

was never enforced and was declared illegal. It still scared many Chinese people that they could come that close to being deported. Even the white Californians who defended their Chinese neighbors most often did so on the grounds that the United States and China needed to keep good relations, not because of human rights.

In 1882, the United States Congress passed the Exclusion Act. It was the result of many years of anti-Chinese sentiment. In the Exclusion Act, a Chinese manual laborer—anybody who worked with his hands—was barred from entering the U.S. It didn't matter whether they were skilled or unskilled laborers. Miners were also specifically banned from entry. The Chinese people who were here already were not allowed to become citizens.

The Chinese people wrote letters of protest to members of Congress and to the community at large. But for the most part, they just kept doing the jobs they could do. It was harder to make a living, but most managed.

In 1888, Congress made things even worse for the Chinese Americans by passing the Scott Act. The Scott Act said that any Chinese person who left the United States temporarily could never come back. About 20,000 men were now stuck in China because of this law. They had been visiting family members back in China. When they tried to return to their homes in the United States, they were denied entry.

The Scott Act also said that Chinese men could come into the country if they had proof that they had a wife, a child, or a parent in the United States. Merchants, preachers, teachers, sailors, journalists, and wealthy travelers were all allowed to come to America with their families. All other Chinese people were banned from coming.

Chinese people became understandably upset over the Scott Act. Their attempts at challenging it in the courts went nowhere. Since most of the immigration officials at the time were concentrated in the major sea ports, some Chinese people tried to come into the United States through Baja California and other parts of Mexico to avoid immigration officials.

Then, in 1892, Congress passed the Geary Act. This act required Chinese people living in the United States to register with the government. They had to carry cards that said they were legal residents. Today's green card laws require all foreign workers to be registered and have cards, but the Geary Act was only limited to Chinese people. Any Chinese person who lost his card could be deported at any time.

This time, the law was outrageous enough that the Chinese community acted. First, they refused to register. Out of the 106,668 Chinese people known to be in the country, only 13,242 of them registered for cards. With so much disobedience, it was hard to enforce the law.

Next, the Six Companies got together to fight the Geary Act. They raised $60,000 to challenge it in the courts. Everyone who heard of the challenge assumed that the Supreme Court would find the Geary Act unconstitutional. Therefore, they were surprised when the Supreme Court did not strike down the law. Many Chinese people felt discouraged by the ruling and felt their rights were being ignored.

In the 1890s, large cities were passing their own laws about Chinese people and jobs. The most popular law was that Chinese people could only work as servants. This is where the stereotype of the Chinese laundry came from. Many Chinese people were forced into jobs as gardeners, laundry-men, cooks, and "house boys" because those were the only jobs they were allowed to have. A few were allowed to start Chinese restaurants.

ANGEL ISLAND

When we think about immigration, we often think of Ellis Island. But the place where most Chinese immigrants arrived was the Angel Island immigration station in the San Francisco Bay. Chinese immigrants were kept on Angel Island until one of the officials was satisfied that they could enter the country. Sometimes they were kept there for months or even years, only to be sent back to China again.

Immigrants were segregated by sex on Angel Island. They had to sleep in triple-bunk beds that were crammed into small buildings. Food was sometimes spoiled, and diseases spread easily in the cramped conditions. Sickness only increased the likelihood that someone would be sent back to China.

The immigrants got frustrated with being kept on Angel Island. Some of them carved poems in Chinese characters on the walls of their dormitory buildings. Most of the poems dealt with captivity, frustration, and loneliness. One young woman even hung herself to demonstrate against the American government's poor treatment of Chinese people. Angel Island was supposed to be the gateway to America, but it was a horrible experience for most immigrants.

To enforce these laws, the police checked up on Chinese people as they left Chinatown to make sure that they had white employers. *Vigilante* gangs also hassled Chinese people. They would beat Chinese people who ventured outside Chinatown. More and more, Chinatowns began to resemble the Jewish *ghettos* of Europe. People were not allowed the choice to live outside of them.

In 1999, the People's Republic of China celebrated the 50th anniversary of Communist rule in their country, with around 500,000 people participating in ceremonies and a parade. These Chinese soldiers are marching in a parade to celebrate this anniversary.

By 1920, many Chinese people had either died or been frightened into going back to China. The Chinese population in America plummeted. The ones who remained had survived vicious attacks. Sometimes, they were branded like cattle, with hot irons. One of the most common ways to humiliate a "Chinaman" was to cut off his queue. A queue was a long braided pigtail worn by all Chinese men. The emperor had originally mandated it, but then queues became a sign of pride for Chinese men. Chinese men who had become Americanized cut off their queues.

By the second decade of the 20th century, the violence towards Chinese people was not as intense. White people were starting to see that they were dealing with fellow human beings, not animals. They became ashamed of their behavior. Chinese people still faced a lot of discrimination, but they were not *lynched* or beaten nearly as often. Also, they had become a larger part of American society and more familiar with American customs. There were still new immigrants coming into the country, but they had the established Chinese-American societies to teach them how to be American. ▪

HONG YEN (HENRY) CHANG

Hong Yen Chang moved to America as a young man and adopted the English name Henry. He studied at Columbia University in New York. Henry wanted to be a lawyer, but he had to get special permission first to become an American citizen. He completed all of his citizenship oaths and requirements in New York and passed their bar exam. Henry Chang was the first Chinese-American lawyer.

However, Henry was not able to achieve all of his goals. He wanted to practice law in California, where there were lots of Chinese Americans who needed his help. The state of California required all lawyers to have passed a bar exam in one of the 50 states. They also had to be U.S. citizens. Henry Chang fit both of those requirements, but California still would not let him practice law. Henry eventually became a political activist and worked extensively in the Chinese community.

A young ex-soldier poses with his new wife in their U.S. home in 1946. The happy couple met and married in China while the soldier was stationed there in the U.S. Army.

5 Allies and War Brides

With the approach of World War II, China and the United States formed a closer relationship. Japan was trying to expand its empire into parts of China and Southeast Asia. The U.S. and China became *allies* against the Japanese. They eventually fought together against the Japanese in World War II.

In the 1930s, the images of Chinese people in America improved steadily. Writers like Pearl Buck and Lin Yutang published books in English that described the lives of Chinese people. In works like *The Good Earth*, Chinese peasants were shown to be simple, hard-working folk. Some white people realized that there were fewer cultural differences than they had thought.

Another *icon* of Chinese people in American culture during the 1930s was Charlie Chan. Charlie Chan was a movie detective. In some ways he was a stereotyped character, but he was also wise and kind. The only Chinese character who had shown up in American movies before Charlie Chan was the evil and sinister Fu Manchu. Charlie Chan replaced a bad stereotype of Chinese people with a good one.

Before World War II, the easiest way for a Chinese person to get into the country was to be a "paper son." It was legal for the child of a Chinese American to come to America. So when a man visited his wife in China, he would report that his wife had conceived a son during his visit, whether or not she had actually become pregnant. The family would then sell the position of "son" to a young man years later, who could then enter the U.S.

In December 1943, President Franklin D. Roosevelt **repealed** the Exclusionary Act. It became much easier for Chinese people to become U.S. citizens. There were still limits on how many Chinese people could become U.S. citizens in one year, but it was a beginning to a new era of increased rights for immigrants and Chinese Americans.

Many Chinese Americans fought in the U.S. Armed Forces in World War II. Congress passed a "War Brides Act" that allowed servicemen to bring home women they'd met while they were serving their country overseas. All of a sudden, Chinese women came into the country at unprecedented rates. Ninety percent of the Chinese immigrants were female in the years from 1947 to 1953.

Also, the Chinese-American population became much younger. Three-quarters of immigrants from 1947 to 1956 were between the ages of 15 and 44. The previous restrictions on immigration had made the Chinese-American community into aging bachelors. The influx of young people shook them up completely and broke up powerful cultural institutions without even trying.

The Chinese-American culture would never be the same again. Most of its institutions, including all of the clubs and even the powerful Six Companies, were based on bachelor men. Chinese-American women never comprised more than 7.2 percent of the Chinese-

American population before 1947. Because there were few women, children were scarce. But after 1947, women and children came to America by the thousands.

Once Chinese Americans were no longer segregated into Chinatowns, they used their opportunities to become successful, vital parts of American society. Education had been highly prized in traditional Chinese culture, and many Chinese-American parents encouraged their children to study hard to

The daughter of American missionaries who served in China, Pearl S. Buck wrote several books that helped explain the mystery of the Far East to her Western readers. She won the Nobel Prize for literature in 1938.

succeed in public schools. Today, Asian-American young people attend college at higher proportions than any other ethnic group.

With the emphasis on education came rebellion. Some Chinese-American young people resented being forced into a stereotypical "brainy" role. They wanted to be normal American teenagers or pursue

The same actor, a Swedish man named Warner Oland, played both the diabolical Fu Manchu (top) and the popular detective Charlie Chan (right) during the 1930s. While both characters were based in part on stereotypes of Chinese men, Charlie Chan depicted a more positive view of Chinese culture.

interests of their own. The struggle between Chinese obedience and American independence still goes on in many families. However, it has not stopped Chinese Americans from achieving success in the sciences and technology fields.

Science and technology were not the only careers that made the Chinese-American community richer. In addition to more traditional pursuits, farming became a more common practice for Chinese Americans. Improved irrigation techniques after World War II made the San Joaquin Valley in California much better for farming. Coincidentally, many Chinese Americans had already settled there, looking for somewhere to live outside San Francisco.

The Chinese-American community benefited greatly from these changes. They helped some Chinese Americans climb out of their ghettos and into nicer neighborhoods.

The established Chinese community welcomed newcomers, called *xin yin min,* or "new immigrants." Starting in the 1940s, about a third of new immigrants already had relatives in the United States, so it was easier to get established and find their way in this country. That practice continues to this day.

The United States continued to open its borders to Chinese refugees. In the 1960s, John F. Kennedy opened up the United States to refugees who wished to escape Communist rule. This group of people set the tone for a whole new group of Chinese immigrants. They had lived through many hardships and *atrocities* during the revolutions in China.

WILLIAM SHAO CHANG CHEN

As soon as World War II was over, China was thrown into revolution. Shao Chang Chen was a 10-year-old resident of Shanghai when the Chinese Communist Party came to power. His parents opposed the Communist takeover and had to flee for their lives in 1949. When they got to America, Shao Chang took the new name "William."

William Chen got his American citizenship as soon as he could. He used his citizenship to serve in ROTC while in college. First, he got his aeronautical engineering and business degrees from University of Michigan and Auburn University. Then he went through Air Command and Staff College with the United States Army. Chen became the first Chinese-American major general in the United States Army. He was the commanding general of the U.S. Army Missile Command. Chen showed that Chinese Americans could go far in serving their new countries.

Asian American students at the University of California pose at their graduation ceremony. Education is important to Chinese and Chinese Americans alike. For many years students have come from China to the United States to receive a good education. Some remain in the United States after graduation, while other return home to China. Chinese American students are more likely to attend college or institutions of higher learning than are members of any other ethnic group.

6 After the Cultural Revolution

In 1965, Congress repealed the last of the restrictions on Chinese immigration. Unfortunately, the new Chinese government had closed off immigration in 1949. Just as America declared its willingness to accept Chinese immigrants, China decided that no one could leave.

Of course, this did not actually mean that no one left China. First of all, many Chinese had fled to the island of Taiwan when the Communist government came to power. During the second half of the 20th century, Taiwanese immigrants arrived in America on a regular basis.

Many others had fled to Hong Kong, which was British-occupied territory until 1997. In 1965, President Johnson **abolished** the immigration system that relied upon ethnic origins. Instead, immigrants were counted from their country of origin. Twenty thousand people per year per country outside the Western Hemisphere were allowed into the United States. Hong Kong's immigrants were thus counted in the total for Great Britain's immigrants, allowing more Chinese people to come to America.

Finally, there are thousands of Chinese people in the U.S. and Canada today who left mainland China illegally. The People's Republic of China has been inconsistent about whether immigrants are allowed or not. From the beginning of the Communist regime, people with *hai-wai-quan-xi* were considered more dangerous than people whose

NOBEL PRIZES

Two young Chinese Americans met during their graduate studies at the University of Chicago, and their meeting changed science forever. Tsung Dao Lee and Chen Ning Yang were both students of physics theory at the university in the 1940s when they started collaborating. When they had finished their schooling, they moved to the prestigious Institute of Advanced Studies in Princeton, the home of Albert Einstein.

Together, Lee and Yang discovered that one of the basic assumptions of physics, parity, was actually not true. Before their work, everyone assumed that if you watched something in a mirror, all the atomic events would look the same as if you were looking at it straight on. Lee and Yang found some situations in which mirror image particles were the opposite of the original particles. They won the 1957 Nobel Prize for Physics for their work. They were still so young when they won that the journalists who came to interview Lee assumed that he was the son of the Nobel Prize winner and asked if his father was home. Only one other winner was ever so young.

family had stayed in China. (*Hai-wai-quan-xi* means "foreign relatives.") Sometimes the government would loosen regulations and allow people to leave China, but at any moment they could change their mind and close the borders again. Most of the people in the U.S. who came from the People's Republic of China left illegally. They were smuggled in by "snakeheads," like the anonymous girl in Chapter One.

In the late 1970s, the restrictions on immigration were briefly lifted. The People's Republic of China allowed more of their population to

Tian'Anmen Square (top) takes up nearly 100 acres of mid-town Beijing. The square was the site of a brutal crackdown on student protestors in 1989. In the photo to the right, a bloodied student is helped through the crowd after a clash with police.

DAVID HO

David Ho moved from Taiwan to the United States with his mother and his younger brother at the age of 12. The boys' father had already been in America for eight years, saving enough money to send for his family. They lived in Los Angeles, where David enjoyed basketball, chess, and science classes. He was sometimes mocked by his classmates for his poor English, but he persevered in his studies and got to be a fluent speaker within six months.

David went to M.I.T. and Caltech for physics and then discovered his interest in the human immune system. He completed his education at Harvard Medical School and started thinking about the largest epidemic in ages: AIDS. David has spent his career looking for ways to treat AIDS by disabling or destroying the virus. During the late 1990s, he worked to develop drugs called protease inhibitors. These have been successful at significantly reducing the level of HIV in infected peoples' bodies. Perhaps even more importantly, he has worked on developing a vaccine so that no one ever has to suffer from AIDS again.

emigrate. However, these restrictions were fleeting. By the 1980s, there were major uprisings in China, and the government felt the need to demonstrate that it was still secure. The borders were closed again.

In 1981, the United States recognized that Taiwan and the People's Republic of China were politically separate countries. Then the number of people who could emigrate from China doubled, because the two were no longer counted together. The number of worker permits, or visas, given by the government was also increased in the late 1980s.

In 1992, Congress passed the Chinese Student Protection Act, which allowed 48,212 Chinese students who were studying in the United States to remain here and get their citizenship. This act was a direct response to the violence of the Tian'Anmen Square protests. In Tian'Anmen Square, students and others had protested the Chinese government's actions. The government had sent in army troops to kill the protesters. At least 200 protesters were acknowledged killed. The U.S. Congress decided to allow more students to stay in the United States so that they could have their rights protected, including freedom of expression.

Chinese Americans constituted about one percent of the population of the United States at the turn of the millennium. Most of the current immigrants are highly educated and well-trained in technical fields. Some are refugees from Communist China or Southeast Asia. Many were born in the United States and have little do to with their Chinese heritage.

Canada's government refused to keep statistics on race for a long time, considering it an invalid way to categorize people. Now that they do involve race in their census, however, it's clear that people of Chinese descent constitute about three percent of the total Canadian population. As in the United States, there are more Chinese in the western provinces of Canada in relation to the general population; however, there are more Chinese as an absolute number in the larger cities, such as Toronto.

Chinese immigration to North America continues to be vital. Chinese Americans have managed to work through discrimination and violence to become a growing and important part of American life. ◼

Notable Chinese Americans

William Shao Chang Chen, U.S. Army general

Steven Chu, physicist

David Ho, AIDS researcher

Maxine Hong Kingston, novelist

Ang Lee, director

Tsung Dao Lee, physicist and Nobel Prize winner

Yuan Lee, chemist and Nobel Prize winner

Maya Lin, memorialist and sculptor

Yo-Yo Ma, cellist

I. M. Pei, architect

Amy Tan, novelist

Chien-Shiung Wu, physicist

Chen Ning Yang, physicist and Nobel Prize winner

Dr. David Ho, director of the Aaron Diamond AIDS Research Center, pioneered research work on protease inhibitors, which reduce the level of HIV in the body. This allows HIV-positive people to live with fewer symptoms for a longer period of time after infection.

Immigration Figures

The Chinese-American population in the United States

1850	758
1860	34,933
1870	63,199
1880	105,465
1890	107,488
1900	89,863
1910	71,531
1920	61,639
1930	74,954
1940	77,504
1950	117,140
1960	135,000
1970	229,000
1980	894,000
1990	1,645,472
2000	2,816,504

Glossary

Abolish to end the observance or effect of.

Ally one that is associated with another as a helper.

Atrocity an extremely wicked, brutal, or cruel act.

Ban to prohibit by legal means.

Bigamy the practice of having two wives.

Botany the study of plant life.

Colonialism control by one power over a dependent area or people.

Communist a system of government in which a single party holds power and the state controls the economy.

Delegation a group of persons chosen to represent others.

Deport to send someone out of the country by legal means.

Emigrate to leave one's place of residence or country to live elsewhere.

Ghetto an area of a city in which members of a minority group live; often the living conditions are not good.

Hybridization the act of crossbreeding plants or specimens to create a new one.

Icon an emblem or symbol.

Immigrant a person who leaves their country of origin to take up permanent residence elsewhere.

Immoral conflicting with generally or traditionally held moral principles.

Import merchandise that is brought in from another country.

Levy the imposition or collection of a tax.

Lynch to put to death (often by hanging) by mob action without legal sanction.

Patronize to treat in a haughty or condescending manner.

Peddler a person who sells items along the street or from door to door.

Prefabricated having the parts of something made at a factory so that construction consists mainly of putting together the parts.

Prejudice preconceived judgment or opinion about someone.

Prestigious having a commanding position in people's minds.

Recruiter a person who works to increase the number or membership of a group.

Repeal to revoke by authoritative act.

Segregate to separate from the general population.

Vigilante someone who uses violence to enforce his own version of the laws.

Further Reading

About the Chinese Americans

Chin, Ko-Lin. *Smuggled Chinese—Clandestine Immigration to the United States*. Philadelphia: Temple University Press, 1999.

Chinese Historical Society of America. *Chinese America: History and Perspectives*. Brisbane: Fong Brothers Printing, 1994.

Farkas, Lani Ah Tye. *Bury My Bones in America*. Nevada City: Carl Mautz Publishing, 1998.

McClain, Charles J. *In Search of Equality: The Chinese Struggle against Discrimination in Nineteenth-Century America*. Berkeley: University of California Press, 1994.

Sung, Betty Lee. *The Experience of Chinese Immigrant Children in New York City*. New York: Center for Migration Studies, 1987.

Tong, Benson. *The Chinese Americans*. Westport, Conn.: Greenwood Press, 2000.

Finding your Chinese American ancestors

Carmack, Sharon DeBartolo. *A Geneaologist's Guide to Discovering Your Immigrant and Ethnic Ancestors*. Cincinnati: Betterway Books, 2000.

Low, Jeanie W. Chooey. *China Connection: Finding Ancestral Roots for Chinese in America*. San Francisco: JWC Low Co., 1994.

Lowell, Waverly B., comp. *Chinese Immigration and Chinese in the United States: records in the Regional Archives of the National Archives and Records Administration*. Reference Information Paper 99. Washington, D.C.: National Archives and Records Administration, 1996.

Internet Resources

http://www.census.gov

The official website of the U.S. Bureau of the Census contains information about the most recent census taken in 2000.

http://www.statcan.ca/start.html

The website for Canada's Bureau of Statistics, which includes population information updated for the most recent census in July 2001.

http://www.geocities.com/Tokyo/3919

This website provides Chinese surnames for genealogical research.

http://www.chcp.org

The website of the Chinese Historical and Cultural Project.

http://www.chsa.org

The Chinese Historical Society of America operates this website; the society also publishes the journals *The Bulletin* and *Chinese America: History and Perspectives*.

http://www.angelisland.org

The web site for the Angel Island Immigration Station Foundation.

Index

Photo Credits

Contributors

Barry Moreno has been librarian and historian at the Ellis Island Immigration Museum and the Statue of Liberty National Monument since 1988. He is the author of *The Statue of Liberty Encyclopedia,* which was published by Simon & Schuster in October 2000. He is a native of Los Angeles, California. After graduation from California State University at Los Angeles, where he earned a degree in history, he joined the National Park Service as a seasonal park ranger at the Statue of Liberty; he eventually became the monument's librarian. In his spare time, Barry enjoys reading, writing, and studying foreign languages and grammar. His biography has been included in *Who's Who Among Hispanic Americans, The Directory of National Park Service Historians, Who's Who in America,* and *The Directory of American Scholars.*

Marissa Lingen is a freelance writer of fiction and educational materials. She was the 1999 winner of the Asimov Award. She is married and lives in Hayward, California.

DATE DUE